BREAKTHROUGHS

A Memoir of Great Comebacks from Setbacks

Judith Nelson

Breakthroughs
A Memoir of Great Comebacks from Setbacks

ISBN: 979-8-42587-990-5

Produced by: Legacy Driven Consulting & Publishing

www.legacydrivenconsulting.com

Acknowledgements

I want to thank God for giving me the courage to step out of my comfort zone and take a leap by faith on this journey of book writing career.

I also want to acknowledge my sister Sherly Nelson, my brother Rubens Nelson, and my parents, mom Cloucite Gelin Nelson and dad Jean Nelson who encouraged me to continue writing this book. I want to also acknowledge my precious God-daughter Shemaya Joseph, who always put a smile on my face whenever I meet her to spend quality time. I want to thank my Coach Mercy, for believing in me, and the entire Legacy Driven Consulting & Publishing team for doing an incredible job by assisting me every step of the way.

Sponsors

Madeleine Leno

Fifi Theluscat

Hydeleine Joseph

Sherly Nelson

Rubens Nelson

Claire Zee

Wendy Joachim

Nickson Charles

Jackson Joseph

Shemaya Joseph

Micky Gresseau

Jenifer Charles

Derly Jean

Fata Ballah

Rose Carmelle Saintcryne

Pastor Carmelle Fils-Aime

Curlyn Daley

Pastor Mercy Myles-Jenkins

Claire Cregger

Here About the Author

Judith Nelson was born and raised in Haiti. Judith transitioned to live in America at age 19. Judith lives in New Jersey with her husband. Judith is now a graduate of William Paterson University, where she majored in Public Health Education and graduated with her bachelor's degree in May 2021.

Judith Nelson is a Health and Wellness Advocate for health promotion, obesity prevention weight loss management. As a health educator, she helps individuals to enhance and increase a healthy lifestyle using her social media platform and providing one-on-one private coaching sessions.

Judith is the founder and CEO of Judfit Collection, LLC, where she sells fitness gear to women as she is devoted to helping them to overcome obesity through weight management.

Facebook: Judith Nelson

LinkedIn: Judith Nelson

Instagram: @judfitcollection

Email: judia56@hotmail.com

Website: www.judfit.com

Introduction

The purpose of this book is pre-determine to encourage individuals who are facing challenges to continue to remain strong because the light is at the end of the tunnel. This book will facilitate you with key details you need to properly face life-altering circumstances with strategic tactics to address particular obstacles. Everyone at some point goes through (some kind of situation) similar situations one way or another. I wanted to share my life experiences so that you can be inspired by how I faced challenges. I have no doubt that my story will help you to see that regardless of how you will be looking at facing your challenges, doing so will become second nature until overcoming your challenge becomes a reality.

Moreover, throughout the course of life, we will encounter difficult times which is inevitable.

Nonetheless, once you understand this concept, you will be able to train yourself on how to survive and overcome any storm that you encounter shall pass. Do not give up on your dream, and do not let your present circumstances define who you are. Do not forget that sometimes, obstacles are part of our personal growth. Also, use your story to prevent others from making the same mistakes. Allow yourself the grace to heal and restore.

I wanted to write this book to inspire other people struggling to make it to school or adjust to the American school system and lifestyle. Thus, I am writing this book to encourage anyone going through sickness, loss, and financial difficulties to not let life circumstances redefine who you are. You've got to let go of whatever it is you need a break from, not because you want to, but because you are unable to continue.

Nothing can take away what God has in store for you, because everything you need to succeed is trapped inside of you. I strongly believe that God gives people another chance for a good reason, because He can take your broken situation and turn it into the most inspiring story. Therefore, you owe it to yourself to forgive yourself, and have the grace of giving yourself another try again. I promise you, if you align with your goals and position yourself to win. Remember, everything happens for a reason, either to help us grow, or to teach us a lesson. If you went through or are still going through a challenge and don't know how to start over or recover, this book is for you as a positive source of inspiration.

Contents

CHAPTER 1

Who am I?

I am the sixth of seven children. I was born and raised in Haiti. My parents, my sister Sherly and my brother Rubens both reside in the USA. I am a health and wellness Advocate, Certified Care Manager, Patient Care Technician, Certified Home Care Manager, Certified Child Care Provider and as well as a Public Health Educator. I am the CEO and Founder of Judfit Collection, LLC.

I would like to share some background information with you about myself. My family and I migrated to the USA in May 2009 when I was 19 years old. Coming to the USA was a little bittersweet, because not everyone in my household was able to come due to age differences and the law in the United States about entering the country with official documents to be legal. To be separated from my siblings was not easy. I constantly missed them, remembering our time growing up in Haiti.

I am a three-time top winner at my church's singing competition in my hometown. The competition was knowledge based, just as it is done nowadays in pageant competitions. The competitions I took part in consisted of a variety of questions such as Biblical, history, music interpretation, History, art, etc. The music aspect of the competition was very competitive; all of us who were participating sang the same song. Whoever made the best interpretation won. It was fun, and we were being ourselves and enjoying being young. After being the winner three years in a row, I chose not to participate anymore so as to leave room for other youth in the church. I received a lot of scholarships, allowing me to participate in any event the church was doing because of my qualifications.

Additionally, I was a public speaker and I occupied a role as a class advocate when I was in middle school at institution of Lavoisier. I learned to speak English from my professor Roody Dorcelus, who invested a lot of time teaching me and my brother Rubens back in Haiti. I also learned intermediate Spanish from Professor Abraham which now helps me to be more open to multicultural, and appreciate others culture. Having learned these two languages helped shaped me into a person with confidence today. Because of multilingual, my personal business line has scale tremendously because I was able to speak different languages and meet my customers' needs. I was always eager to learn and would participate in any competition my school held. Therefore, pursuing my passion for languages pushed me to learn to speak English, French, and intermediate Spanish.

I was well-known in my community because of my personality, talent for singing, modeling, and public speaking. However, there was other aspects of my childhood that was traumatic to live. Even though, there was something I was not aware of an early age, but as I got older I started to question myself about them and analyzing the root cause of the issue.

One of the reasons I said that my childhood was traumatic at some point is because, being born biculture with a dark complexion in Haiti was a big deal in my community. I don't see any value on stigmatizing color. When I was growing up, I was compared with my other siblings and was made to feel different. Now I embrace my complexion I am different to stand out for who I am, and that what's makes me priceless. I never allowed people's opinion to define who I am nor did I allow them to convince me to bleach my skin to fit in. However, I took into great consideration when someone make a statement. I faced many challenges from my childhood, kids will try to bully me because I was a chubby girl. The first time that happened, I defended myself by fighting them back. I was that quiet kid in school but I was not the one who will sit and let the kids do whatever they want with me. I went home and told my mom what had happened. My sister Kerby had a plan to tell the kids in school that I was a twin with my brother, because we looked alike a lot. The plan worked out well, the kids started to pull back and left me alone. Although a dark time during my childhood was part of my story, there was something deep inside that made me stronger from time to time. It was like feeling the future before living the future.

In this book, I will take you through my life journey; where you will learn a lot of information about me. I am from a biracial family. My grandmother was originally from Dominican Republic, and my grandfather from Haiti. I picked up a few words of Spanish from my grandmother, which helps me a lot when I went to school in Haiti to understand the basic Spanish words. This part of my story was the hardest part for me as a child, to understand racism at a very young age. It was so clear and loud, it has become the new normal thing that people will say or do. It was obvious they would make difference between the light brown and dark brown complexion to me which as discriminating. I remember vividly when discrimination was a common issue in many households in the nation during my childhood. People gave more attention to the child with the lighter skin. Yes it was hurtful to see how others was trying to make me feel bad for having dark skin. Then I came to my senses at 8 years old, making up my mind to confront anyone who will speak negative about my skin. I spoke openly about it, and letting them know that there is no kids with lighter skin that was better than me. That is when I started growing my personal development skills. At 8 years old, I already knew how to do my hair nicely. I would practice on my mother's hair. Before I knew it, I became the most famous kid in the neighborhood because of my talent to hair braiding. The people no longer saw my dark complexion. I had kids and adults lined up for me to do their hair. I became an entrepreneur then. I did not charge them for doing their hair because at that time, I was proving something to them that was more than money. That is when they started to bring gifts and goods to my house in gratitude. I was not allowed to take a vacation to visit my beloved family in Dominican Republic because of my complexion, while other family members could travel to the Dominican Republic without any difficulties. Even my aunts and other people in the family would travel there in a heartbeat. But my mother always told us that we would get killed if we traveled. Therefore, I never knew anyone from my grandmother's side. This was the worst feeling I had to endure as a child, and it create nightmares in my subconscious. I became aware that discrimination was so cruel. This situation caused me to grow up with a sense of disdain, and fear of Dominicans because of what I went through. As I became older, I realized that the issue was more of a political matter than a personal bias opinion. See, Haiti occupied the Dominican Republic from 1801-1844. This has created a lot of political tension between the two countries. This realization helped me to turn my thinking in a different direction by not holding onto hate for things that I did not create nor could change suddenly. Instead, I started developing love and appreciation for cultures and diversity. I want to be the change breaker. I want to use non-violent resistance to resolve complicated issue (Dr. Martin Luther King). Knowing that love surpasses all form of negativity is a tool that could bring tremendous change in the world.

I migrated to this country in 2009. I was born in a family of eight children. My oldest brother was born a twin, but unfortunately, the other twin, who was a girl, did not make it. She died shortly after birth. Now, seven of us remains. Three of us are currently living in the USA with my parents. My oldest brother

Billy, is living in Chile, and my three sisters are living in Dominican Republic due to political terror in Haiti.

This is a very difficult moment for me and my family. Knowing how Haitian's are being treated badly in Dominican Republic. This breaks my heart!

I came to the USA because of my uncle Andrew, who filed the immigration paperwork for us. My father never wanted to travel to a different country; he was comfortable where he was at that time. My father was a well-known professor at Lycée-Petion, the most prestigious state college in Port-Aux-Prince, where he taught Greek and Latin. He was also a student at the same school, before becoming a professor. My dad earned his Ph.D. in Literature and proceeded to teach not only Greek and Latin, but also English in Haiti. He was also blessed to be knowledgeable about Math, Spanish, and History. My father was born into a family of three children, where he, my uncle and my aunt were fortunate to have the financial freedom to travel to any country of their choice.

Nevertheless, because their mindset was focused on farming, my family was considered among the people who had the largest portions of real estate in our city. I can remember traveling 20 to 30 miles away by a donkey with my dad to visit his farm.

Due to the large number of crops they grew and the amount of money they were making, traveling was not interested to them, which for me, was the worst mistake they made. Even my dad was making a lot of money. He could have traveled to see other part of the world and learn new concepts of farming.

Work Experience

A family with five women is an interesting one. There was a rule in my family that the oldest was supposed to support and take care of the youngest. Meaning, the youngest eats first in a situation where there is not enough food. The oldest sister was responsible for grooming, feeding, bathing, and cooking when my mother was not around. We were assigned to each other in that way. There was a cooking schedule, a cleaning schedule, a laundry schedule, and a schedule for food shopping. By taking responsibility within the household, we grew up with a good work ethic from my mother's side because her job was more physical than my dad's. We had a lot of good time together, we entertained ourselves by enjoying with music. We dance together, we cooked and wear each other's clothes. It's such a beautiful thing to be able to have siblings. I and my siblings always got each other's back.

Growing up in a family with a good work ethic, I started my self-employed job at the age of nine. This happened when I was a child. I always wanted to have a new hairstyle every morning when I was going to school. I remember my sister Kerby used to be upset when she had to get up and do my hair. Often, the hairstyle she gave me was not ideal. You know, not looking quite right. As a result, at nine years old, I asked my mother if she could do me a favor and buy two mirrors for me to use to learn to do my own hair. This is how I started my first business. After I was proficient in doing my hair, which took about three to six months for me to learn, I practiced on my mother's hair, as well as my sisters'. I became so good at it. I started braiding kids' hair from my neighborhood, and in return, their parents would give me goods such as clothes, sandals, etc.

My second job was teaching for a Swiss business owner who lived in my city, La Tremblay. Every month, I made $300, which in 2007 was a good amount of money. I was a personal tutor who helped his niece with general homework, as well as teaching her basic English. That job was a great fit because it did not stop me from going to school. I worked there from 4pm to 6pm. At the time, I was about 18 years old and I was teaching a beautiful kiddo name Mina, who had difficulty in school. Therefore, it required a lot of patience to teach her. She struggled to memorize anything you teach her, and in particular, had trouble remembering anything anyone taught her visually. The job was not easy, but because I was committed to helping her, I created my own approach to teaching her.

One method I used was showing her that she was not a bad student. I smiled with her, I taught her to be confident, and encouraged her to not be too afraid to say whatever was on her mind, even if it was not the correct answer. Over the time, she became more open with me and confident. She turned into a brilliant girl smiling and chanting while repeating her lesson. I was overwhelmed with joy to see how far she came, from not having any confidence to being the most joyful girl I knew!

The second teaching strategy I used with her was nodding my head. When we were doing her reading assignment, I nodded my head as a sense of reassurance that she was doing a good job, that she could keep reading more.

I found my third job as a full-time teacher at a preschool while holding on to this private job. The teaching aspect of both jobs made me felt accomplished. I felt that way, not because I was the best at teaching but I was blown away to observe a student who started from having a hard time in my classroom to now being able to stand out. I have known that I have a sparkle of love in my heart for children even since I started these jobs. I chose these jobs, because I love children, and I have that connection because my school years as a child were not easy. I was not one of the fast learners in school. I had difficulties catching up with the rest of the class because every year, I barely had two or three books for the school year.

My third job was working at a middle school where I taught kids from two to four years old. This teaching experience changed my life; I really felt I could make an impact on the kids' lives. One story that touches me the most was when after three months of starting my teaching career, one of the parents testified how her son, who was not able to learn, was now doing well in school. Before the arrival of their parents, I usually started teaching the children about the lessons they would need to recite in class. My class was always on point with décor and presentation, and my students were learning well.

My fourth job was supervising students at a sewing school, where they were learning how to make clothing. This experience was very inspiring. It enabled me to gain more leadership skills such as good communication and personal development.

I was also a part of an intellectual club "Cadec," which was a place young people came to learn how to occupy leadership roles in society. We met every Sunday, and we had different departments. Some of us were specialists in dancing, poetry, and public speaking. I was in public speaking and singing. In my church, I was also part of the church youth and adult choir at "New Jerusalem".

I quit teaching when I left Haiti to come to the USA in May 2009. After I arrived in the USA, I began to seek new dreams and challenged myself to break through barriers of limitations.

***

Before driving on my own, I used to catch the bus on Ocean Avenue to get to work. Then in the morning, my brother pick me up since he was the only one who had his license at that time. After five months of my brother picking me up, I decided to study to take my driving test in Bayonne, New Jersey. During this process, I studied for the test in French because it was easier. I registered to take the test on a Friday. The first time I took the test in French, I did not pass. From that point on, every time I took the writing test, I failed. I never realize that taking the test in French was that difficult. It was not until I figured the way I was translating English to French was not an ideal thing to do. Every time the computer shut down, I knew my time was over. I was shaking when, walking over to the Receptionist's desk.

What encouraged me the most was when I went to get my testing result. There was a very cheerful and caring white man at the front desk who was supposed to give me my result. He looked at my paper and told me, "Ms. Nelson, you are almost there. I believe you can pass this test. You did ok, but you missed few questions and didn't quite get a passing score. I want you to go home and rest, then study so you can come back again next Friday." He may not know how much these words of encouragement helped me, but it was everything that I wanted to hear.

One reason I struggled with the test, first is that I studied in English and took the test in French. The second problem was, in Haiti, we studied differently. The test structure was not the same. I could remember studying in my home where I had to memorize word by word everything in the book, but this testing system was different.

I finally passed the writing part, which I took almost ten times.

I was working at McDonald's, and I could not afford to buy an expensive car, so my first car was a 1996 Honda civic, which I bought for $500 from a family member. Just by the year of the car, you can picture it as old and broken, but buying it was a great accomplishment that I was proud of. The driving process was not easy, being that it was my first car and the first time I was going to be driving. That time for me was a chance to build momentum to prove to myself that I can be anything that I wanted to be. I used the downfall of failing the tests as fuel to help me in different areas of my life to remind me, that I've got everything it takes to make it to the next level.

I was not permitted to drive after 6pm for the first six months after receiving my license, so I had one of the family members who were available at that time to take me to work with the car because my job started at 10pm. Then they would drive the car back home, and I would have my brother pick me up at 5am when the streets were the most dangerous because of people who were doing illegal activities. The driving process was not easy and this old car started to give me one problem after the other.

All these experiences taught me that the journey in life for one to reach their goals is sometimes both bitter and sweet. There will be distractions, life events, bad people, and difficult events.

Hope is the capacity of seeing the good and the imaginary dreams comes true. What are you hoping you have the power to do today? The question is asked intentionally because once the desire is in your heart, the next step to making your dreams come to pass is applying your knowledge and experience to your life. For that to happen, you will need to pair your hopes and dreams with discipline. Therefore, it is vital to keep hoping and visioning everything you want to do and want to become, until you get into the habit of doing so. You may have the greatest dreams and visions in the world, but without implementation, you will never get to your destination.

Furthermore, whatever desire is burning deep inside your heart, let it come out. Remember, when you are going to start, not everyone will believe you can be or do what you set out to be and do. Know that the intuition you have is real. Write it down, pray about it, and find out how you can perfect it. Now, while you may find people who believe in you or not, I want you to keep going no matter what because often, you may not see the value in an idea right away. It may not make sense. But as you open yourself to possibility, there will come a time when the ideas will flood in your spirit, and you will be astonished by the transformation they bring.

Choose Faith over Fear

Faith is the action of believing in something even before it happens. Faith will serve you as fuel in times of uncertainty—when you feel down and want to give. Know that deep inside, if you can give it another try, your situation will not be the same. Faith will force you to be more realistic. Even seeing your vision through prior experiences will help you put your dreams into action. For example, believing that sitting down in a chair that will not break is faith. Now, say that you sat down and the chair broke down. This may give you a spirit of fear the next time you will need to sit. But would you remain standing all your life because you are afraid another chair will do the same, or are you going to take a leap of faith and sit anyway? Some of you reading this right now may choose to remain standing for the rest of your life because of fear, and some of you may say, "I don't think all chairs are going to do the same thing. Let me give it a try." Well, the choice will always be yours to make at free will, but keep in mind that with every decision comes with consequences. That is why I urge you today to take a leap of faith towards your desires to accomplish your dreams. I want to assure you that the beginning will not be easy, and that goes for every one of us who wants to take the road to success. But five to ten years from now, you will be so grateful that you took that step forward. Stepping forward is an opportunity for growth; it will stretch you to the next level.

You must have a **Roadmap** that you create and that will help you to stay focused.

- **Boldness** - I highly recommend is to ***think with boldness***. Do not be afraid to push yourself beyond your limits, for it is a stretching exercise that will improve your personal development and self-growth.
- **Write the Vision** - I recommend is to ***write down your goals and dreams.*** Put them on your nightstand, in your bathroom, on your refrigerator door, and even in your car as well as in your office. Anywhere you know that will capture your eyes. It will make you rediscover yourself; it will also help you to evaluate your progress through self-assessment.
- **Inspiration** - This book, which is my first book, is a perfect example of ***leaping by faith***. ***I am believing in myself that***, after writing this book, not only will a lot of lives be changed, but I will also ***inspire others to do the same***.
- **Imagination** - When facing dark times, ***use your imagination*** to envision yourself overcoming challenges. See yourself through; see yourself out!

CHAPTER 2

Adapting to the New System and Culture

Adapting to a new culture is a transition a lot of us must make in our lives. Transitioning to another country could completely change your life. Sometimes making a change is something we do willingly, and sometimes life circumstances push us towards making changes. Living in a country for 19 years demonstrated that I had been accustomed to a lot of cultural customs and a particular lifestyle. When anyone is exposed to a new venture, they are both happy and worried at the same time. These contradictory feelings are a normal part of the process.

For me, arriving here in USA and being left to navigate the school system alone without having someone to help was the hardest part. What made it special was that starting from struggling with school—even the whole school system—was very difficult for me. In my case, since I was eager to make new discoveries and was ready for what laid ahead. I embraced the high and lows of my new life with confidence.

Relearning English and the School System

Anyone who's used to their native language for a long period of time will find it difficult to transition to a new language. Nevertheless, this happens to stretch us so that we can develop in many ways. Relearning English in a new environment is not easy, especially when someone is older. Everything I learned in Haiti was not easily transferable, but my English skills helped me to get by in my day-to-day life here in the USA. My English professor, Miss Vera, a very kind woman from the Philippines, encouraged me to spend time reading more books as well as watching Channel 13 to be more familiar with a lot of words. Doing that gave me the foundation that helped me to gain confidence that even if I spoke with an accent or not, I had the boldness to speak even if I felt like I was not speaking the language perfectly enough. I knew basic English from back home, and it seemed that it was a good start. However, I noticed the difference was, the people spoke more rapidly.

But I was conscious that people were thinking about me speaking with an accent. I had to face reality and embrace myself for who I was. In fact, after accepting myself, I now feel like speaking with my accent takes me back to who I am, and I am proud of it.

In Haiti, when I use to speak English with my classmates or my professor, it was different. We spoke at a slower speed and some of the words are different. Trying to speak English in the USA exposed me to a broader aspect of the language and forced me to improve myself.

Hospitalization of my Mother

Difficult times will surely come, but with the right focus, one can thrive while overcoming every single obstacle. We may encounter situations that shape our characters and cause us to become a better person; as a result of these situations, we may change for better or worse. When something is going on in your life. Never have the intention of cutting to the chase of things. Take the time to study the situation, then you can move further by analyzing and making wise decisions.

My family and I migrated to the USA for a better life. My goals were all laid out in order. I set a timeline for myself to start school and to purchase my first home—doing the things that people called "The American Dream". I created my vision board, I prayed about it and worked hard toward achieving my goals.

Turns out, life has a lot of hidden surprises. If we are not wise and driven, we will question our ability to become the best version of ourselves. How do you handle life when you face one crisis after the other? When all roads appear to be closed off to you? When everything you touch turns against you as if it was some sort of bad luck? Well, that was my situation. I never had time to go on a vacation because if I did, the family would be short for rent money for that month. My siblings and I were all in school at the same time and working for minimum wage. We tried to cover the family responsibilities, so that my mother wouldn't feel like she was helpless.

And so we covered her expenses so she could stay home. Despite her age, she wanted to go to work, but knowing her health issues and how the workplace may treat her, we decided to pay her every time we got paid so she didn't have to work. Unfortunately, 2009-2011 was a very difficult time. I went to school from 10am to 6pm, and after that, I went to the library to read and study with my brother. We were in the same school and even the same classes together. We attended the school for a year and in May 2010, we both graduated with our GED.

Coming home from work when my shift ended at 6am was somewhat of a challenge. By the time I reached home, it was already 7am. I slept between one and a half hours to two hours per day at that time. I was so focus on what was essential that some days I didn't even had a chance to sleep, not because I didn't want to sleep, but because I could not sleep due to overwhelming family needs. One thing about me is that even if I went to bed, I wouldn't be able to sleep if I had worries on my mind. I would go drop my mom at her babysitting job, and after that, I would drop my sister at school and go do laundry or food shopping before returning home. Then I would sleep for two hours before getting up and getting ready for school.

In 2009, my mom started to feel sick. My mom was spitting up blood, but not a lot. When she asked to see a doctor, my cousin said, if she brought my mom to a doctor, the bill would fall under my mom's name. My mother came to the USA with a permanent resident card, but because we did not know much about the health care system. After a prolonged complaint, my cousin's husband decided to take my mom to the doctor.

Between 2010 and 2011 was when my mom's health challenges began to worsen. My mother was having chest pain, and later, she started to spit more blood. Later she was bought to a clinic for evaluation. The doctor prescribed her some medication. Gradually, the bleeding decreased, but after a few months, she started having different symptoms which she had to go to Jersey City Medical Center for. When she arrived, she was told by the doctor that she was going to need a defibrillator. We did not know what the procedure was, and my mother was afraid of the news and denied the procedure.

The period between 2010-2011 continued to get worse. I was working at Burger King at that time. As usual, when I got up around 5am every day, my mother was usually up because that was her regular time to go to work when she was back in Haiti. Suddenly, I felt something was wrong; she was sitting on the chair very early between 5–6am. She went to take a shower and sit down. I asked her, "Mom, are you ok?" She said no, she said she felt hot. That is when I knew something was seriously wrong. Since she did not appear as if it was an emergency, when I asked her if I should call 911, she said “No”. I asked my brother to take her to the hospital.

One thing I did not really like about my mother is that my mom never showed us when she was in pain. If I wasn't persistent, I wouldn't get any answer from her. The reason being is that growing up, she was always the main source of providing for the family. Telling us she was sick would show signs of weakness. She was always strong and was constantly fighting to make sure things are taken care of.

My brother got up, took a shower, and headed to the hospital with my mom. Thanks to God, Lord Jesus, my mom made it just in time before her heart stopped. The doctor shocked my brother when he said my mom's heart was so deprived of oxygen that, if she had stayed in the house for a few more minutes, she would have died. But God was faithful to us all the time.

My brother Rubens told me that right away after she got checked in by the Receptionist for chest pain, they took her immediately. Jersey City Medical Center is a very good hospital that takes its patients very seriously. I was there once for chest pain and they took me right in, right away.

After my mother entered the emergency room, they performed emergency surgery on her. She was then sent to the critical care unit (ICU) for her major heart surgery. She was diagnosed with heart failure. This news devasted my heart because my mother was all I had. She always made a lot of sacrifices to make sure we were fed, and she maintained a lifestyle of prayer;

praying every day, 24 hours around the clock since even before my brother was born.

The reason she kept that kind of lifestyle is due to a demonic spirit that was attacking us when we were children. (I will further explain this story in my second book. Just stay tuned for that. It will bless you abundantly.) Anyhow, through it all, God remained faithful, He never left our side. My mom prayed the whole time she was in the hospital. As usual, she was always on the phone praying with her friends.

Back in Haiti, we had a house of prayer where people came from all over the town to pray. We sometimes received visitors coming from the USA, Canada, etc., coming for my mother to pray for them because she was gifted in the areas of healing and deliverance.

Her hospital stay was a very dark moment at every level. My mother did not trust doctors. We are from Haiti, and most of the people in Haiti do not often go for doctor's visits unless it's a real emergency that occurs. Therefore, the nurses and the doctors in New Jersey had a very difficult time with her. She would not comply with taking the medication. Remember she had heart disease so taking her medication was very important for her.

Struggling with School and Work

While my mother was sick, I was a full-time student at Essex County College and so were my sister and my brother. So, because my mother refused to take her medication, we had asked the doctor if we could come and stay with her to see if her anxiety would decrease. My mother also heard of many incidences that happened in the hospital regarding the doctors being after the money instead of wanting to help the patients. So, I had to balance my schedule between my sister and my brother so we could take turns staying with her in the hospital. We rotated our shifts from time to time; my brother would do the night shift when I had to work at night, and my sister took over the evening shift. After leaving work, I would go directly to the school, and from school, I would run home to take a shower and head to the hospital in less than 30 minutes.

Come the day of my mother's surgery, her doctor mentioned that she needed to have a pacemaker based upon her situation. So, my brother and I were there at that time and we asked the doctor a lot of questions. Thank God my mother had sent us to an after-school program back in Haiti so we could learn English! Funny, it was the three of us children who were fluent in English that moved to the USA.

The medical staff came to take my mother after we signed the paperwork. We were told that she had a 50 percent chance of survival. My heart almost stopped because I could not afford to lose my mom, so I stayed in her room while she was gone for the surgery and prayed for her.

One of the medical staff came to ask us if my mom used to speak a different language because as they were operating on her and we were praying fervently, the Holy Spirit came down, glory to God, and my mother started to speak in tongues, which the doctor could not comprehend.

I am saying this to encourage you for when you are going through some stuff that you and the people around you can't understand. Focus on listening to God, who said that in due time He is going to come to visit you. And when the fullness of the Holy Spirit visits you, people will be shocked to see that your story is going to change. In fact, your name will be changed in the same way God changed Jacob's name to Israel. I pray that if you are reading this book right now and you are going through some hard times that the holy hand of God touches you right where you are, in Jesus's name, Amen.

After the surgery, I was going back and forth to the hospital. While I was in class, the nurse from the ICU called me. They informed me that our mother would be left alone. I had tears in my heart coming out of my eyes, and continued praying to God for a miracle. Because of the nature of her health and people's mentality who were close to her, she was not given much chance to survive. I asked the hospital not to accept visitors because if other friends or family came to visit her, they would tell her things she wouldn't want to hear. You know the devil is a liar. My mother told me one of the staff members who was Haitian told her she was most likely not to come alive because many patients who came for the same procedure did not make it. When my mother told me that, I was extremely mad to the point of wanting this lady to be fired. I had a chance to meet with her, and I spoke very harshly with her because of what she told my mother. I wanted to report her to the director of nursing in charge. My mother wouldn't let me do it. Afterwards, I found out this staff member was related to someone who went to the same church we went to. The lesson in that story is that sometimes, it's people who know who you are who are trying to destroy you. Be vigilant and stay in prayer so God can give you discernment.

While my mother was in the ICU, she could not do anything for herself, so I made sure everyone treated her well. Being that I was in the medical field, I would help the Nursing Assistants when they came to help my mother, and sometimes when I was not tired, I would just help my mother on my own.

At that time, it was a lot of back and forth from the hospital to school, from school to work, and so on. Sometimes when I was in class, the doctor was calling me to ask me to tell my mother that it was ok to take the medication. I was overwhelmed. Sometimes the nurse would call and say one of us had to come to the hospital immediately. They could find an interpreter to translate to and from Creole for her but, unless one of us was present, my mother would not take the medication.

I remember falling asleep while commuting one time during this period. When I was working in Weehawken at the ferry terminal for Central Parking, I took the light rail to and from work. I heard someone was yelling, "Miss! Miss." Turns out the light rail had arrived at the last stop, and I was sleeping deeply. The train driver had mistakenly returned to the train station with me still asleep on the train. So, I apologized to him and explain why I was sleeping on the train. It was around 1am, so he headed back with only me on the light rail. From the station, I was 30 minutes from home and by myself. It was scary!

Despite what life throws at you, stay strong. I know it's not going to be easy but do not quit. The situation you are in right now will soon end. When that happens, do not forget to encourage someone else you know to go through the same pain.

Meanwhile, my mother was sent home from the hospital. Every night was a battle. My mother could not speak, so we put mini stones in a bottle so every time she made noise by shaking it, we knew she needed help.

***

No child can ever finish repaying their parents for what they have done for them. One thing that has served me as fuel is knowing that I'm doing this for them and doing it for the glory of God. The focus it takes to support a loved one is very rewarding as well. This draws my attention to how sometimes God can use us to be public servants to others. God can use us to serve our family. If you are in a similar situation where you are supporting your parents or supporting your siblings, do not think of your task as a burden. See it as an assignment that God has placed on you. It could be to empower you and shape you into a better person for a higher purpose. God want us to serve in Jerusalem, meaning within but also outside of your family.

Challenges with School

Transitioning from high school to college was not an easy process because I did not go to a regular high school due to my age. My brother and I attended an adult day high school in Jersey City. After finishing this program, we started to attend Hudson Community College in fall 2011, where they put me into a program which placed me in an English class for two years. Both my brother and I passed those classes. The advisors at the college told us we could not move forward in the program without taking all these classes, which sounded not too good for us. Due to my mother's health situation, I dropped out of Hudson Community College to work three jobs to take care of my mother. While working at the healthcare facility as a Care Manager, I found helping other sick people to be a basic thing that we may take for granted. Knowing the nurses were taking care of my mother while I was working to help other patients like my mother was a very rewarding experience. My job at that time, I did not know where the church was. All I knew was, I was interested in going back to school. I completed the program at the church and then I went on to apply for Essex County College.

In addition to that, God sent a wonderful woman on my mothers' path just as I was about to start school. Her name was Mary Day. My mother met her just at the right time. The amount of support and help she invested in my mom was too true to believe. I personally looked at her as if she was an angel sent by God. I love and appreciate all her decimations to be by my mother's side. She came into my mother's life in due time.

I did not know how I was going to navigate working three jobs and going to school while also caring for my mother. The sad part about my mother's sickness is that she was not able to stay by herself. During her sickness, my dad was living in my cousin's house, so she was alone along until Ms. Day took my mother under her wing. She took care of my mother like she was her own mother. I said to myself, "This can only be God."

Ms. Day was a Nurse, thank God. She would check my mother's medication and make sure my mother was covered. One of my mother's medications was making her heart beat very fast—to the point where we had to take her to the hospital. When Ms. Day reviewed the medication, she found out my mother was prescribed high blood pressure medication when she did not need it. She immediately stopped taking it.

I entered Essex County College in 2013 while completing my Patient Care Technician certification in New York City. I registered for 12 credits, and at that time, I was working as a Nursing Assistant per diem at one job. I floated from floor to floor since they were not able to give me a proper schedule because of my school schedule. This job was my first job in the Health Care Industry. While working 40 hours along with going to school full-time, I pursued my passion.

To continue with my education. I was being charged $2,000 each semester for being out of County. I had to pay extract out of my pocket. I decided that was too much of a burden for me. I transferred to Essex County College from Hudson County College so I could avoid all the additional tuition. Living there, I was able to take English classes along with other classes.

In 2016, I graduated with my associate degree in General Science. At the same time, I was working to pay for my education and care for my parents. I did not qualify for financial because I made $13,000 a year. After graduation, I was eager to start the nursing program, but I felt in my heart I was not meant to go for Nursing. I prayed about it and could not get admitted to any nursing program. I went to few colleges but I did not pass the entrance exams because I could not get into the nursing program. Therefore, I did not continue with another major and I took another year off. I worked full time, and was still out looking to go to a nursing program.

God knew I wasn't going to be able to work as a nurse during this pandemic. Due to my underlying medical issues, I was praising God during the lockdown for not letting me go into nursing. Right after I decided to go to Public Health, my advisor asked me if I was a nursing major and I said I was. He replied, "You have all the requirements. I don't know why you were not admitted."

The best is yet to come. God has a reason; He does everything for a specific reason.

CHAPTER 3

Re-hospitalization of My Mother

Deep inside of me, I had a feeling that something was wrong. After the first surgery, my mother was visiting her doctor who had done the surgery on her. When he was calling her to come in, he told us that nothing was wrong with her because we were paying cash. Otherwise, if he had done some examinations, he would have discovered something was wrong. So, when she returned to the hospital, the same doctor came to introduce himself again and informed us he was the one who was going to do the surgery again. I stood up and refused his request. I told the person in charge of the floor if they could not find another surgeon for my mother, we would have her transferred to another hospital right away. So, they contacted another surgeon. That is when Doctor Barber came and requested that no one else touches my mother.

Just when meeting the doctor, I saw that he was caring and compassionate. After the second surgery, I took my mother to his office so he could check on her. He was by far for me one of the greatest doctors. Sometimes, when I had to run to school to do an exam, he would take my mother in and manage to speak with my mom. Surprisingly, my mom said she loved the doctor because he was patient with her.

At that time, her medical bills were not being paid by any insurance. I had to pay out of pocket, and sometimes my whole check went into buying medications. I can remember one time walking into a Walgreens when the pharmacist told me that the cost for me to pick up the medication was $300. Her doctor's visit was $500 per visit, so I had to be accountable for that visit because my brother and my sister, who lived with me, were not making enough money from their jobs to help me cover the expenses.

So, I called 911. They got her to the emergency room, and they found out that the previous peacemaker had been incorrectly installed. Because of that, even though the first surgery was not completely healed, they had to cut her open again in the same spot.

The room they put my mother looked and smelled like death. I did not like how I saw her; she looked like someone who would be sent to a nursing home for recovery, but that is when the impossible happened. After long hours of praying and crying before God, as my brother, my sister and I united in our faith, God showed up in my mother's room. Shekinah of glory came down to remove what the enemy wanted us to believe.

A few days passed by and my mother was still at the hospital. To God be the glory, the medical staff saw my mother's situation was at the point where she shouldn't get up to go to the bathroom. They gave her bedpans to do her needs. But God said, "No, my daughter, you will not die. You will live to declare the glory of God." The atmosphere changed. Her face was glowing and the pain was going away gradually.

I declare, if you are reading this story right now, I release healing over you. I release breakthrough over you in Jesus' name, Amen.

Financial Struggle

I used to work as a hairstylist in a studio where I rented a chair, but there came a point when I told myself I need to do better for myself. I started selling products for Avon as a distributor and was willing to do whatever I needed to do to make more money to help myself financially. At that point in life, after trying and succeeding in some new ventures and failing at others, I learned that you are never too old to learn nor too young to teach. My financial struggle at that time was a problem but I never let it get the best of me. Because of my creativity, I knew there would be something I could produce of value that would help me make more money. I came to know that money is good to have, but not all we want to have. One must also seek wisdom, which will empower you to do better when you know better.

How to Survive Financial Hardship and Remain Focused on Your Dreams

Financial hardship is a lack of financial resources; one has due to lack of information or inability to properly navigate through a system. Financial troubles could also be the result of the inability to create. I am saying this to activate something.

The USA is a place everyone knows has a lot of opportunity. But for those opportunities to align to you, there must be a pathway to follow so that you can unlock them. While you are in a crisis, do a needs assessment. Ask yourself, "What do I have available to me right now that I can use to create more income?" It could be something very simple as knowing how to cook, braiding hair, being a comedian—anything you can think of that could help you thrive. Do not be afraid to try whatever skill you have until something happens. Believe it or not, once you shape your mind to align with your passion and make it a habit, you will become unstoppable. The process is not going to come easy; there will be highs and lows, which is all part of the process. Remind yourself that you must be strategic in how you spend your money. You need to be able to differentiate what your needs are versus your wants. Your needs are that which is necessary for you to have in your present moment, and your wants are something you want to have, but they are not a priority. Therefore, you must map those things out on a paper or in your mind so that you do not overspend. In fact, your spending needs to be lower than you're earning.

I use this strategy and it works for me because, when I was working for $7.00 per hour, I had to decide how I was going to spend that money. I couldn't just buy nice clothes and leave my car with no gas. I like beautiful clothes, but the gas was a necessity that couldn't wait. I had to make critical decisions like that. When I started working here in the USA, there were times when I could not afford a brand-new pair of shoes. I had to go to Salvation Army to shop for clothing.

One time I had only $10 to shop for clothes to attend a church celebration. I bought shoes for $3, a dress for $5, and a purse for $2. And when I tell you, I washed them and put them on for the event, you could not tell I purchased them there. My circumstances did not define me, because I knew where I was and where I wanted to be. I've gone from not being able to buy new shoes to now to having multiple pairs of brand-new shoes.

While you are going through trials, keep your guard up. Do not blame yourself or someone else. Just try your best and be appreciative for the little that you have. Don't allow peer pressure to make you feel insecure. People in your circle who see you but do not know who you are will project their insecurity onto you, whether by showing off for talking in a certain way. When that happens, do not give an answer; give notice. Be sure about yourself and have the courage to face life with confidence. Unless you do so, you will find you are never happy, you never have enough, and most importantly, you will live your life following a crowd. You were born to be different. Do not allow society to label you.

I use to be in the situation where I had to choose between eating or feeding my mother. That moment alone changed my entire world. It gave me even more determination to have a reason to fight. I used to spend days with no food. Sometimes, I would go to school at Essex County College from 7am to 9pm, with no food. I remember not being able to find where I parked. I was dizzy, hungry, and tired, and yet the next day, I would do the same thing over and over again.

One moment I can vividly remember was going to the food court and grabbing something to eat. I went to the register and pulled out my PNC card. The card did not go through. I told the lady that I was coming back but even up to today I never went back. I felt so humiliated and left the food at the counter. Deep in my heart, I was hurt, and water could not stop running in my eyes. I sat down, and told myself that was the last time something like that would happen to me.

This took me back when I was in Haiti. I used to go to school without food, and the students thought I did not want to eat because I was too cute. I never told the students my business, even the one who sat next to me. I was very secretive because I felt ashamed.

Childhood

Growing up, I would often question my existence. I never understood why I had to grow up in a family that was dysfunctional. I never comprehended why I could not go to the

Dominican Republic simply because I was Black. My family's name was the so-called big name, but we were suffering in silence covering up my father's mess. In his church, people knew him for his title, which is no wonder. No one could talk to him to reprimand him for his evil behavior. I disliked my father since I was eight years old after he had a heated argument with my mother. I felt bad for my mom; she did not deserve to be treated that way. I told her that she was too kind to my father. I developed such a deep hate for that man, that I told myself all men are the same. I refused to take commands from any man that was in the family.

But, gosh, I feel better now, and I see male characters differently. My feelings towards my father have affected my romantic relationships; I made a lot of biased assumptions about men. And there were some relationships that carried pain and bad experiences.

In 2008 or so, my father called all of us into a meeting. I was excited. I thought maybe he was going to send one of us overseas to study or something because he had made it clear that no one should miss the meeting. He arrived and sat down. The breaking news was that he was so overwhelmed with us, because he had spent so much of his life taking care of us that now that we were grown, we needed to figure a way to survive on our own. I was very upset and wished I had never been born in such family. My world fell apart; I was confused and worried.

Since I was involved in church activities and Christian activities in the community, I was open to start looking for a job.

One day, when I was on my way to school, I heard someone calling me, "Ms., can I speak to you for a minute?" I kept going without even looking back. I never like when strangers are calling me, so I did not pay attention to him. He was dressed in fitness gear and had a radio in his hand.

A different time, I saw the same man at the intersection where we both had to pass by. He stopped and introduced himself and said that he always saw me going to school very early every day. He said he was an English professor and he also worked as an interpreter. He said that he was working on a filming project and asked if I knew anyone who may be interested in attending.

This happened few months prior to my being offered a job to work as a teacher in a school. At that time, in 2009, the first thing that hit me was what my dad had said to us. I used to perform in church, as well as in a community outreach club for young people. I also enjoyed singing and had won multiple awards. As a student, I took the liberty to be early in school because I did not like when class started without me. A lot of time, I left home without eating my breakfast so I could be on time to catch a taxi before the 7am rush hour. This man invited me to a group meeting. He said I would meet with everyone who would participate in the movie. He showed me the script and said that it was a movie that was compatible with 'The Titanic', which I had heard of but not seen.

When I went to the place he told me, I did not see anyone. So I asked, "Where are the rest of the people?" He answered, "They are running late," so I started to leave then he said that they were coming the following day, so I went back the next day.

I told one of my sisters about the role and the movie opportunity, hoping it was something that could help me have access to travel and work. When I arrived the following day, he said that he was going to give me my script to study while others were coming. And that is when he molested me. I was virgin, and I was bleeding.

I was so scared, and I went home after he had said something like, "Now, I'm your boyfriend." I was so confused and felt so stupid for not understanding that he had intended to molest me. This event really destroyed the joyful talented Judith I knew. It sent me on a lot of detours and heartbreak.

My parents usually said that before any of us get married, we need to focus on school. But I never had a chance to have any of my parents explain certain things a teenager needed to know. They had only mentioned, "Don't have a boyfriend, focus on school and church." That was the norm.

No one in my family knew about the molestation. I choose not to say anything about it because my mother was traumatized by what she was going through with my dad and my aunt, who made her life a living hell. I told myself that telling my mother about that would be enough to kill her. I became very angry and started to have a complete behavior changed.

I struggled with this for years. I never forgave myself. I use to hate my father with a passion. I was very rude to him whenever he talked to me. I could not control my anger for him. Seeing him around the house irritated me all the time. I never felt like I was living in a home. I felt like a stranger living in the house. At that time, I never saw myself marrying to a man anytime in the future since my father was the worst role model of a male figure.

Before all this situation, I was always someone with very positive energy.

I wanted to be married one day and have a beautiful family, but the hurt I went through was bigger than those dreams. I remember wanting to hear that my molester died. Then, I heard a voice speak in my mind saying, “Do not worry, I am going to handle him. You don't have to wish him to have died.”

After few years, I had a vision where I felt in my spirit that he was punished for what he did to me. I could not understand why I was hearing this voice. It lasted for a few days, and then I started to feel healed.

After a couple of years, I found a pastor who was preaching on YouTube about forgiveness. I told myself I could forgive someone who did something else to me but not this monster. Then, I continue listening to the pastor. To tell you the truth, I did not agree with everything he was saying. His name is Pastor Gregory Toussaint. He was saying that unless you are healed from the wrongdoings that other people did to you, you will never be healed, and the devil still has access to make you feel that you are not worthy. After the molestation, I felt like there was a void in me. It was like someone had stolen something very precious from me and I didn’t know how to get it back. Regardless of what I did, it was hunting me down. After the sermon, I started doing meditation. I prayed day and night about it until God took away the pain.

I could not find it in my heart to forgive my father because to me, he is too wicked, evil, and unworthy to even have a child. I told him that one day, I used to burn his clothes when he left to go to downtown Port-au-Prince. I would burn anything that I found that was his. That is how I showed my anger toward him. I prayed about my anger and asked God to explain this verse that says, ***"Children obey your parents" Ephesians 6:1 (NIV).*** I asked God, "How about the parents that don't deserve to be treated with respect?" The answer was very simple. Although obeying him or respecting him may not be something he deserves, do it for the glory of God and let God handle the rest. I came to realize that the hate and the pain were going to make me bitter towards him, myself, and others around me. I decided to map out a process to let go and let God take over. Trust me, it was not easy; it took me almost ten years to completely forget about his evil doings.

The Power of Forgiveness

Forgiveness is, by definition, the act of letting go. One way or another, we all have been in situations where someone else has hurt our feelings or we have hurt people. How does one acknowledge the necessity of forgiving?

The Lord's prayer do answer this question for us. In ***Matthew 6: 9-13*** it says that ***"Forgive who trespass against us".*** It is a powerful prayer. When you forgive, you are not forgiving the person because they deserve it. Instead, you forgive them for the sake of your peace and for you to have a clear conscience. Did someone hurt you, betrayed you? Ask God to give you a forgiving heart today so that you can find in your heart the grace to forgive. Find the courage of letting go, and let God handle it. By doing so, you will live happier, and healthier.

Forgiveness can heal your soul, and can aid to find peace, restoration and transformation. Every time you have a chance to forgive, do it without hesitation. It may not be the easiest thing to do, but it surely is the right thing to do.

Challenges during Secondary School

During my school years back in Haiti, it was a fun thing to go to your friend's houses to meet with their parents and get to know them. Parents back home would not send their children to your house unless they knew your family or knew you personally. So, I could remember visiting my countless classmates' homes, but they never came to my house. It is a very sad story, but I embrace every part of it. I could not believe what was happening to me, but it is what it is. Students were not welcomed in my house because I went to their houses and saw how great their parents were to us, and how well their house was put together, which was a very good thing for a parent to do for their children. In some instances, there were students whose parents would not afford to build a mansion, but they had what they could afford. I am saying this not because I was jealous of how their house looked or anything. The part that I constantly asked myself was, "Why does my father have to keep us in his grandmother's mud house and never have any sense of urgency that there are five female children plus two boys growing in the house, yet we only have two rooms to share?" This idea aggravated me to the core, because my father was a real estate investor who purchased homes to rent to other people. In total, my father had five or six houses he was renting, to my knowledge. I strongly believe he had more than that.

I felt so embarrassed just remaining in the family, sometimes asking him why he even had us when he knew he was going to be that wicked. Not only did he treated us badly, but his evil sister was also the author of all his evil deeds. My father was not a giving person; he never liked when we had friends over. He complained about everything.

When I was ten years old, my professors would come to my house to visit. This is a common thing they do in Haiti, which, in my opinion, is not a bad thing. Most of them came because of my mother. My mother is the most caring person I know on earth. She received people in the house with open arms. They use to call her "Manman Nels." My mother is a Prayer Warrior who prayed 24/7. I used to ask her, “When do you have a break?” It is now that I realized that she could not get a break, or else all of us would have died because there was a strong evil spirit on both my mother's and father’s side. The worse part about it was that, even though my aunt was a churchgoer, she was a witch at the same time. She would try to kill us with voodoo, but because my mother was praying, God did not allow her to harm us. Every day, my mother would have a prayer service at home where sometimes 50 to 100 people used to show up, and other times, there were more. My house used to be a house of prayer. My mother built a separate house to receive sick people who were suffering from demonic attacks. Some of these people stayed for one year; others stayed for longer. One of the sick who was extremely ill had died in the temple of prayer. People who knew my mother loved her because she was a humanitarian. Individuals from the neighborhood used to come and ask her if they were allowed to take lemons from our garden to go sell at the supermarket, and my mother would grant them favor with no hesitation. Two of my best friends were able to come to my house because I was comfortable to openly talk to them about my family background.

2019: Another Difficult Year

Living in America now, I encountered a terrible experience that negatively affected my mental, physical, and emotional health. On my way to work, I was in the intersection and another car ran into my car. I was injured and suffered a back injury, concussion, and neck pain as well. Right after the accident happened, I remember seeing the other driver running across the street with two other individuals in his car. Someone called 911. And my head was hurting so bad that I could not speak. I was immobile, waiting for the ambulance to come. They towed my car, and I was taken to the hospital. I could not speak, but I was able to call my sister and give the phone to the doctor so they could talk to her and let her know that I was injured in a car accident. I was in a lot of pain and in the same month, I was supposed to take a state exam for medication aide. I had to cancel the test by calling the health department. However, I was diagnosed with a concussion that day at the hospital. After being released from the hospital, I went home, and that is when the pain started to worsen.

I entered university to continue my semester, which was the last semester before my graduation in May 2019.

I discovered the educational material would normally take me more than five to six hours as opposed to two to three hours expected to learn the material. That is when I realized I was having trouble focusing on school. In one class I was taking, "Public Health Practice", I failed the in-class test and my professor started questioning me because she knew that I was in her other classes before and in comparison, now I was not doing well. My professor suggested that I go to the department in charge to ask for help. As a result, I went to the advisory department in the school to explain what was going on. I was assigned to a mentor, David, who walked me through the process of healing. He was phenomenal. I was delayed in my goal of graduating in 2020, so I waited for the following semester to go back. This experience taught me a valuable lesson about life. No matter what life throws your way, with consistency and keeping your goals in mind, never allow your circumstances to define who you are.

I was in-denial in mid-October. I did not want to redraw from school because I did not have a lot of time left to complete my semester. My health was declining time after time. I could not believe my mentor told me to drop out to rest because my eyes were very sensitive to light.

I went through a lot of therapy to see if could recover. The therapy was not enough. Therefore, I was sent to see a neurologist to do further testing. Because I was suffering from extreme headaches, I was given multiple narcotics medications, but the side effects were not ideal. After the back and forth to the doctor, he gave me a letter to bring to the school stating that I could not continue studying. After several counselling sessions, I finally decided to drop out. It was in March 2020 when the pandemic happened. I then realized I was not going to be able to go through the intensive studying along with doing an internship.

Sometimes, it is not worth questioning a situation that you cannot change. The best option may not be the right option, but if it is what is good for you at that time, do it.

Graduating College with an Associate Degree

Although I was taking care of my mom along with my siblings, I was so blessed to have Ms. Day to provide her support by picking my mother up every morning before we went to school, and bringing her back when we were off from school and work. She did all of that without charging us not even a dime! I do not have any words to explain of how grateful I am towards her.

In life it is important to treat others the way you wanted to be treated. During my time working in health care since 2013, every time I have a bad day at work, I remind myself of what she did for my mother. It has stuck with me ever since—to pass on the good others do for me. Because of her kind help, I was able to graduate college.

Becoming Unhealthy and Obese

Working nights at McDonald's, dropping my sister off at school and my mother to the babysitter, I was so busy. Sleeping for two hours per day did affect my health. Not only was I eating the food from my job and working overnight, I was not getting enough sleep in order for my body to even repair itself. As a result of that, I gained such an excess amount of weight, which caused me to feel tired and have knee pain all the time. One moment that changed my life is when a fellow co-worker told me she was going for a knee surgery. I sat for a moment and thought to myself, "I cannot continue living like this." That is when I started taking healthy measures to improve my health. I never had a chance to prioritize some time for exercise, because of lack of awareness I had about my risk of becoming sick and being exposed to preventable diseases.

While working at the McDonald's, as a start, I made a plan to get some certifications from a trade school that could help me sustain myself during the time I was going to be in college. At the same time, while working at McDonald's, I was saving mostly $30 from every pay check to put aside for the nursing assistant class. I worked at McDonald's for a year and a half. In the meantime, I went for my security license. After receiving my license, a family friend referred me to Central Parking. I used to work on the cruise ships in Bayonne and in Weehawken at the ferry. Most of the time, I was working at the ferry station because it used to get very busy there. I worked there as a cashier and enjoyed the company of my co-workers. I was getting paid $9 dollars per hour in 2013. I went to school for my Nursing Assistant, and Certified Home Health

Aide certification. After one year, I went to school in New York City to complete my Patient Care Technician certification.

By putting all my efforts on personal growth, I went from not being able to buy a pair of shoes to being able to make a $1,300 pay check and $300 to $400 overtime pay. I decided to focus on my personal growth and help my parents here while supporting family members back home. Anyone who is willing to go through the process will be able to overcome any fear of getting out from your comfort zone.

Loss of Employment

In 2016, I was working as a CNA while pursuing my dream of becoming a registered Nurse, although, there was two majors on my list that I wanted to do. It was either Nursing or Law. My experience after my mother's illnesses drew me to the nursing field. I went on studying general science just in case I did not get in the nursing program in the school because of the waiting list, I could study something else. In November, I got injured at work. I was in excruciated pain. I had a herniated disc and a bulging disc. The job sent me to their doctor. He did an exam and he told me that nothing was wrong with me but I was in pain all the time. I knew something was wrong. Regardless of what I told them, they did not admit that I was unable to work. They had me doing lifting, and I was doing a lot of walking back and forth. I went to a lawyer's office, they took the case, and after few weeks, the lawyer called me and told me there was a conflict of interest and that he couldn't take my case. One of the people working at the law firm was handling another case for the facility.

He referred me to another lawyer and I transferred to work with them. For some reason, I had a gut feeling that the lawyer was on the facility's side instead of mine. She was forcing me to settle the case while I was sick. I removed her from my case. While I was doing therapy for over six months, the therapist referred me to another lawyer. When I found out where the lawyer was from, I knew she was going to do a good job. She made sure I got all my treatments and took matters into her hands. This did not stop the job from firing me, because I was going off and on to the emergency room, and that was a loss for them. Every time the pain got worse, I went to the emergency room to get a shot for the pain. I lost my job. I filed for unemployment, but the process is not something that is done in one day.

During that time, my brother and my sister weren't working enough to pay for the household expenses on their own. We used to put our money together to pay for rent. But being that, I used to make more money but when I got sick, the income decreased. We paid our rent as we could, but sometimes if they didn't have the rest of the money, we gave what we had to the landlord. And I personally explained to her what the situation was. She filed for eviction the same week I had the court appointment to receive my unemployment. I paid her and left the house. She was in shock when I told her I was leaving the house.

Graduating with Bachelor's Degrees

My sister Sherly attended William Paterson University in spring 2017. She inspired me to change my career path, because I was so determined to do nursing until I found a program that would take me in and until I passed the nursing entrance exam. I couldn't stop trying. One thing I realized during the course of taking the nursing entrance exam is that, when I failed these tests by two to three points the first and second time, and the third time I tried, I failed by six points. That realization got me thinking about changing my career even if I wasn't 100 percent ready to give up on nursing.

Soon, I learned that being obese was going to be affecting my life because I had knee pain every day at work and after leaving work to come home. I also learned that being in the field while my mother was sick was very helpful because I was able to pass on the same caring and compassionate care that the nurses had given my mother while she was in the hospital. But nursing was not for me. I quickly realized that if I continue with nursing, I would have trouble standing for long hours to work due to knee pain and back injury.

While my sister started one semester ahead of me majoring in Public Health Education, I was curious as to what she was taking. I researched the program and saw that Public Health Education was not much different from nursing. I would have the flexibility of working from home on my laptop, as well as the freedom to travel to interact with people within the same scope of practice. I was interested in signing up for that. So, I went to the school to inquire about it, and I got accepted the same day because I already had an associate degree in General Science. I was not prepared to pay any registration fees, but they told me that I needed to pay $120, which I did not fully have on me. Thank God for good people, the Cashier at the school told me not to worry about it—that he would add the rest. (I was short by about $5 or so.) I did not plan to start school right away because, at first, I didn't know I was getting accepted the same day.

My first semester at William Paterson University was a great experience. I knew what to expect because my sister had already taken these classes. However, I had decided not to use any of her information. I did not want to become the type of student who was copying and pasting.

The first semester I passed all my classes with mostly A's and some B's. Remaining in class was not easy because I was on heavy narcotics medications, and it was hard to focus in class while in pain. There was a time when I fell asleep in class because of the medications. I could not remain seated for more than 20 minutes. I constantly got up to walk and come back to the class. The situation prompted me to sit in the back of the class, which is never my favorite place to sit. As a student, I always preferred to sit in the second or third row, but not in the back. I know not many students like to sit in the front, especially some friends I met in college. But sitting in the front pushes me to make more effort to know the material, and when the professors know that you know your stuff, they usually leave you alone. Back in Haiti, I liked to sit in the first row or third because I had to write down everything the professor was saying.

My father never provided us with all the academic materials we needed in school, not because he could not afford it, but because he accepted his sister's dictation to him as to how we should live and how much of what we should have. Her control really made me and my siblings have a very terrible childhood.

Anyhow, the pain was so intense, it was like a sharp object that was cutting my lower back and my sciatica nerves were hurting me every time I stood up to walk. It was also like a needle was poking me. In wintertime, I was like someone who was breathing and physically present on earth, but I felt like I was like a dead person. The pain made me feel depressed and stressed out. The worst part about the pain was it was non-stop. The only time that gave me a little break was when I would lie down in the bed. Picture me lying in bed for most of the time when I was not in school. Without any physical exercise, I gained over 100 pounds. Now imagine, despite the pain, I had to spend at least 5 to 10 hours studying and doing homework per day. Keep in mind my major was slightly like nursing. So, this added more pressure on my spine and on my back.

Besides that, stress normally affects muscle on your back, adding to the back injury. It was not easy at all, but I had this burning desire to finish what I started. I did not have any option to take a break. I developed my own strategy that fit my needs. I took a break in between; I prayed, I meditated, and I spoke to my inner being that with and without pain. I was going to push through. I was fortunate to be able to find a private study room which my sister, her friend, and I could use to do study groups.

When the pain got more intense when I was in school, I would bring a small blanket with me to school so that I could use it to lie down on the floor in a private room. I had started school with no car due to the car accident. My sister and I had a different schedule, so even though she had her own car, I could not go with her because by the time my classes started, I would have been sitting too much. I took the bus to school every morning at 5am in order to make it to my 7am classes.

I was placed in a program in school called Arc. It's a program that helps students with disability. At first, I denied accepting that I had a temporary disability but I had to admit this was the case when I wasn't able to focus at all in school. This program helps students to study at a lower speed and is non-discriminatory.

I could say the staff members at the school—the hospitality staff and my professors at the Public Health Department—were by far the greatest people I ever met during my time in school. Dealing with them reminded me of when I used to volunteer at the hospital in Jersey City Medical Center back in 2013, where I served patients as if I was working as a regular staff member. I also volunteered at the veteran courthouse, where I was helping with doing civil engagement.

These experiences humbled me in a way that makes me serve other people with a kind heart, knowing that regardless of our background, all of us are human and deserve to be treated equally. Nevertheless, this does not mean that I did not face discrimination in school from white professors, but, because my mindset and focus were greater than the hate that was thrown at me, I kept going and made them appear invisible to me.

The Benefit of Being a Public Health Educator

Becoming a Public Health Educator for me was the best decision I could ever make. It enlightened my understanding more about the risk factors associated with obesity. It also enabled me to think about my current situation deeply and pushed me to take more action towards my health. My mother's current health status made me want to go out of my comfort zone to improve my own health.

My mother is now living with a defibrillator as well as a pacemaker, which she recently changed back in January 2021. The third surgery was really scary being that my mother is aged and was not feeling well. She had lost so much weight that we were so afraid that she may not come back but we had no other choice but to trust God in the midst of everything.

For the surgery, my mother moved out of New Jersey to go reside in Boston. I went to Jersey City Medical Center to get all her medical records, which her doctor in Boston had a hard time retrieving from the hospital. Sadly, the hospital mistakenly forgot if my mother was allergic to anything. The nurse had everything ready on the table to give her, and suddenly, the Creole translator was running late, they had no choice but to ask me to translate for them. When I got to the room, the first question the nurse asked me was if she is allergic to any medication. I told my mother what the nurse said, and she did not even remember she was allergic to anything. The nurse was so shocked because the medication my mother is allergic to would have been the first thing she gave my mother. I was shocked too, because I told them she was allergic to it, but mistakenly it was not recorded on her chart.

The lesson to this is that sometimes, God can delay your path for your own good, but you also need to have the discernment to know if it's the voice of God or if this is coming from the devil.

CHAPTER 4

Gifts

Reset

Hitting reset is necessary as it allows you to assess and re-evaluate your life. Often, you may find yourself in a situation that you put yourself in and realize that you are unbearably overwhelmed. Remember to take a deep breath, pause, relax, and think. Make sure that you ask God to give you a calm spirit. Pressing on is worth it when facing a difficult time and something is worth pursuing.

Other times, you just need to assess the situation and let go. Remember, every mistake that happens to you does not make you a failure. Learn from them, grow from them, and use your mistakes to teach others about your experience.

Resilience

Resilience is a virtue that one has that is served to elevate oneself when facing a difficult time. The urge to remain resilient is evident more than ever. First, you need to know how to become a resilient person. Becoming resilient is not something that will be handed to you. Instead, it is a virtue that you will develop as you are going through a process called growth. With growth comes wisdom, and with wisdom comes stability in character.

For example, you may be struggling with school and work while taking care of your kids or your parents. You do not give up because you know what the cause of your sacrifices is. You are envisioning getting this degree so that you can then find a better job. By having a better job, you can change your financial situation and your social status. You keep fighting until this vision becomes a reality. Along the way, you develop what we call inner strength.

Resolve

Resolve is the action of finding common ground to solve a problem. Do you find yourself in a situation where you do not know what to do? Well, there is a solution. Maybe you do not know how to solve your problem, or who can help you solve it. Suppose you find yourself having a language barrier to communicate effectively. Try to learn the language, read a lot, and do activities that can help you engage in speaking. You may consider joining a community club or develop self-learning material.

Respect

Respect is a law that is reciprocated if you are respecting others and they do not respect you. There is some sort of imbalance somewhere. Make sure to speak up for yourself.

Respect is earned not given, make sure to align your character that give notice of your personality and who you want others to see you for and treat you for. Ask yourself this question, '*Are you doing what you suppose to do to earn that respect?* ' There are variety of question you can ask to find the answer, however, by the end of the day, you are accountable for what happens to you when it comes to how people are treating you.

Be mindful also of your surroundings. The type of people and energy you attract to your environment will determine who you become. '*What kind of attraction does your energy bring?*" Ask yourself this question that no one else will be able to answer for you. Be honest to yourself.

Release

Release is the action of giving in if you will be giving something away. Releasing your emotions helps you to let go of things that are hurting you deep inside your subconscious. Do not bury them, and do not pretend that you have gotten over them and are healed. Face reality for your peace. If you must pray, pray. If you need to call someone to make peace, let it be so. If you must hold a family meeting, go for it. Seek for peace. Release yourself, free yourself.

Forgive those who hurt you, not because they deserve it. Do it for your peace.

CHAPTER 5

Steps to Get a RESULT

Strategies for Coping

I have developed five steps which will help you to tap into your higher being. I firmly believe that God created you with a unique talent to change lives and inspire the world.

Here are the steps that will help you to unlock your true self.

Step One - Seek Counseling

Seeking counseling is one of the hardest things for someone from the Caribbean, especially for anyone born and raised in Haiti. Seeking help, gives you clarity and helps you re-evaluate yourself to be guided in the right direction. Often, it is sporadic to see an adult deliberately speaking to someone about things they are going through as a usual conversation. Depending on what weight the family last name carries, people suffer in silence and even die because of depression instead of getting help. As simple as it seems to ask for help, when it comes to health issues such as life and death, in my personal experience, I must force the other person to talk until she can tell me exactly what her problem is.

Seeking counseling is not bad. It allows you to express yourself and ask for help when you need it the most. The lesson here is that everyone must start from somewhere because starting a new life in a new environment should not make you feel like you are not good enough. Consider yourself a resilient person in the first place. You may have to learn to adapt to new environment. That does not mean that you are not enough. Learn to validate yourself, embrace yourself, and learn to accept your imperfections. Parts of your life you may see as imperfections are otherwise strengths, because after you develop that area of weakness, you become a better version of yourself.

Another way to get access to a counselor is by asking for help in your local community. There are federal organizations in place to provide counseling to anyone who needs it.

Try to know the language to the best of your ability. Transitioning to a new environment is never easy, but with your willingness to learn, everything will be possible, you just have to believe in yourself and trust the process. Remain faithful, for it is my confidence and faith that you will be able to survive any difficult time. Turn your story into empowerment. Do not allow it to defeat you. Make a conscious decision that you will use your story to impact the world. For you never know whose life your story will touch.

Step Two - Surround Yourself with Positive People

Positive people have natural energy in them that can change your atmosphere by changing your thinking. When you are around someone positive, their well-being can elevate your soul and activate your thinking to a different route.

Someone positive will always give you hope and strategies to overcome dark situations. Therefore, connecting with people with a positive attitude will make you want to change even if that was not your intention.

Why am I saying all of this? I am saying it because only someone who sees farther than you can give you constructive advice and help you to grow. Find yourself a positive and energetic spirit to be around. Surrounding yourself with positive people forces you to believe it is possible to change from negative behavior to healthy behavior. Ask people who are from the same background as you if they have experienced something like what you are going through. Ask them what they do to cope with the situation.

Step Three - Set Healthy Boundaries

Setting healthy boundaries is when you can confidently explain why you are doing or not doing something. You can do so calmly and appropriately without causing any harm or destroying your relationship.

Another way to set healthy boundaries is by knowing what your needs are. Once you know them, convey them to the person so you and the person can be clear on what to expect from each other. For example, when you go into a hiring process, the person interviewing you will give some verbal information about the company's core values as well as some written information. In some instances, they will have you sign some paperwork to acknowledge that you have read and understood everything written on their papers regarding rules and regulations. Teach others to value your opinion and show them that you are serious about your position while being open to constructive criticism. Always do what is right and fair for both parties.

Step Four - Self-Evaluation

Self-evaluation is vital to consider when thinking about improving oneself. We need to expose our inner strengths and weaknesses and allow ourselves to be vulnerable to find healing. According to its original definition, in social psychology, self-assessment is the process of looking at oneself to assess aspects that are important to one's identity. It is one of the motives that drives self-evaluation, along with self-verification and self-enhancement.

Learn to Say No

Learning to say no is the ability to decline an offer or a request made by someone. Suppose you are finding yourself in a situation where you cannot say no, even if you are unable to fulfill a task, you agree to overload yourself with promises you cannot deliver on a timely manner. This will disqualify you from many occasions in life. Learning to say no is not a bad thing, it means you know your limit on what you can proficiently achieve or not. Next time your boss, friend or your co-worker are forcing you to do something you are not comfortable to do, kindly decline the offer in a polite way. For example, your boss ask you to stay to cover a shift, and that day, you were not able to do it. You can rely, '*Dear Lora, thank you for asking me to stay, but I need to pick up my daughter at the daycare. Please, let me know in advance so next time I could plan accordingly.* ' You can also say, '*I am running to go to my next job as soon as I am done here. I could stay, but I have another job from a proposal made by a friend, employer, or family member.*' It is time to seek help. Countless times, we feel like we are being taken advantage of, whether it is at work, at church, or in a relationship, and we even feel bad about it without acting.

Not only should you stand for yourself and take defense, but it is also essential to not allow others to take advantage of you. Do not let anyone take your kindness for weakness. If you are unable to manage your actions and do not put limitations on how much of what you can offer someone, you will find yourself in a situation where you feel like you are obligating to do it for them. People will use that against you and use it as a way of manipulation. Be mindful not to confuse that with selfishness.

Some individuals cannot say no just because the request comes from a close friend, husband, or wife. You may feel uncomfortable at first, which is ok. Take a deep breath and find the strength to say no. Remember, saying no is not wrong person.

Sometimes, individuals do not say no because of pride. You may feel like you have all the power to rescue the world when you do not. When you do that to yourself, you are adding a task unto yourself where you know deep inside your heart that you cannot respect it. Avoid over promising and under delivering. If you have to be received as weak just to protect your peace, let it be so.

Earn Your Story

Earning your story is very important to find inner healing and being able to inspire someone else. One must be able to identify solutions. You may not look like what you have been through and what you are continuing to go through. Nevertheless, if you find yourself struggling to heal, you need to tell yourself a story and the lessons you learned from it. This signals to yourself that you are healed—you're whole again—that your experience does not define who you are.

Remember, everyone has a story to tell. Your story is not too small, and it is not too ugly to hear. Sometimes, things happen to us that are out of our control. Understand that life could happen to all of us. You are beautifully created, you are unique, you are loved, and you are a masterpiece. Remind yourself every day that if anyone can do it, then you can do it too. And if you can do it, you can surely activate someone to be encouraged to do the same.

CHAPTER 6

Knowing your self-worth is a quality that no one can put a price tag on to determine its worth. When you know who you are, your values and what you stand for, it sets the tone so that even if you are at your lowest point in life, you are confident that you can overcome any situation. As mentioned before, seek counselling and seek help if you find yourself in a situation that you alone are not enough to solve. Talk to a close friend, by all means, do not suffer in silence. Avoid mental breakdown at all costs. You are too precious.

4 Ways to Turn Any Setback into Your Comeback

1. Give yourself the opportunity to start over again.

Starting over in some instances may not feel like the right thing to do at the beginning of the process. But you must start over for the right reason and do not hesitate to do so. Supposed you was driving on a one way street, would you continue driving in that direction knowing that you and others are in harm's way. The answer is no. Preventing the danger is the right thing to do. Now picture the same example for something you are doing in your life that needs to be adjusted. Ask yourself, do you feel like you are in the right path? Yes, you need to do a quick stop and turn around to the correct route. Do not do the right thing for the wrong reason, nor the wrong thing for the right reason according to your personal belief.

Setback Mentality: "*Will I ever recover from this situation?*"

By definition, a setback is a reversal or check in process (Oxford's English Dictionary). So, now which one resonates with you? Some individuals intentionally decide to setback by choice. If the individual makes the decision to do so, it will have a lower impact on them. But when the setback happens involuntary, sometimes it may bring distraction, self-sabotage behaviour, pain and even depression. When we experience life challenges, we can often lose ourselves in the situation, hopefully just for a moment. Setback is sometimes good to help us to re-assess ourselves and see where we fall off so we can pick ourselves back and keep going stronger.

Comeback Mentality: No matter how long I had to wait while on the setback, now you will give it all you got to get up stronger than you ever taught. You are racing the idea of coming back in full force and making it happen. I remember being on a car accident in August 2019, I had just finished a session in school.

In September, I started college full-time. I didn't know the severity of the pain. Turns out I could not perform well in class. I was forgetful. Normally, I excel in my classes, but this time, I could see myself falling big time. I was assigned to a mentor, which was a tremendous help because I did not want to drop out of school being that I had one more semester to graduate from the program. I didn't see that my health came first. I was very disappointed in myself. When I finally give in to drop out, five months later was the beginning of the lockdown which has started exactly on my birthday March the 16th. Looking at my decision to drop out was the best decision because managing the workload of the internship, capstone, and thesis, in my condition was impossible to perform within such time constraints. I knew my health would not allow me to perform.

Sometimes, life happens, and we have no choice but to setback. But while setting back, you may find yourself feeling sad, depressed, confused, etc. The good advice for that is to setback and plan your comeback. Map out your plan by envisioning how different you would do things when you are back on your feet. Train your brain to see the good in the situation, for everything happens for a reason.

Another example of setback was when Simone Biles, a four time-Olympic gold medallist, redraw from participating the Olympic game. She prioritized her mental health which was the best choice ever. This is a good example of a good reason to take a setback to tell oneself, its ok if I am not ok, and not letting society's pressure force us to do something that we don't want to do, nor cannot do for the sake of prioritizing our well-being.

2. **Give yourself permission to let go of what's holding you back.**

Find a way to be in a position where you are bold and courageous enough to let go of the things you no longer have control over. Truth is, the past is already gone. The only favor we can do to ourselves is to learn and move on reminding oneself of the ability to evolve and change. Envision yourself moving forward and living on the other side of life. Speak life to yourself, forgive yourself, and embrace who you are becoming. You are worth it, and deserve to be here and shine, so do not give any chances to the past to hold you back. Your past was a part of your story. Today is a new day so allow yourself to blossom gracefully.

3. **You have everything you need to move forward.**

Coming into this world by birth, God intentionally allowed us to come naked. The reason being, what you need to function effectively is not on what you put on the outside that matters first. It is not in copying what someone else is doing. If so, you would spend the rest of your life living a fake life. God created you to live an abundant life. This means that you will be so successful that your blessings of all kinds will overflow at a level, that you will be fortunate enough to bless others.

4. **Resolve this matter to release this burden.**

The art of resolve and release is so powerful. You must chose happiness over anything in this world, for by being your best self, you will be able to conquer the world.

Use Your Own Story

Using your story is the key to heal yourself. The world needs to know how great of a person you are. Do not allow your downfall to write the script of your future. You will find yourselves regretting not acting earlier, and when you die, you will take all your dreams unaccomplished to the grave. Pastor Myles Munroe explains that the riches place on earth is the grave. It is where people die with ideas, inventions and many things that could have changed the world because they were so scared and afraid, they did not even try to birth those dreams. He was right about that because his death taught me a lesson. He was teaching the world on how to be great and serve with dignity but now he is gone. I would not believe it, I never met him not even a day, but his teachings transformed me. I remember one day listening to his tapes, he said: "You who are listening to me, cannot even afford to pay your gas bills, yet you have a lot of ideas you don't want to put them out to the world. I was so shocked; he was talking to me. One word changed me. Since then, I have decided to double my efforts in everything I do to get to write my very first book today.

If you just believe once again in yourself, you can get up right now and start writing your visions and goals. Unless you have the audacity to dream it, you won't be able to live it. You have a very priceless stressor hidden inside of you. You need to come out of the shadow. Do not worry about who will laugh at you. People will always be there to do just that if they have never been in your shoes. The same way when you are driving a car, you do not look backward. It's the same thing you need to do to go after your dreams. Use your failure as a mechanism to motivate you from going forward. Tell yourself, if yesterday, I was not good at doing this or that, now, I want to invest money, time and resources into myself to prove me wrong. Remember, our biggest enemy is not your neighbor, it is not some of your followers on social media. Your enemy is “You”. Stop judging yourself and start developing yourself. Do the things you wouldn’t do before. Set healthy boundaries. Love on yourself.

Remember you are valued.

Remember you are loved.

Remember you are appreciated.

Remember you are a masterpiece.

CHAPTER 7

Restoration, Prayer, and Inspiration

Inspiration from Life Experience

Life's lessons from facing loss, sickness, injury, and financial crisis and any other storms that you may be going through will eventually pass. Do not see your situation as something that could define who you are. Even in reality, you may feel like everything you touch is not bearing fruits, or you may find yourself in a situation you never wish to be. Despite all, you are still worth living. You are worth getting up and trying again. Truthfully speaking, you only fail when you let negative voices speaking in your head tell you that you are not worth it.

Know that before you were born, God placed within you everything you needed to be successful. Always find your "why". Your why is something that makes you want to wake up every morning and say to yourself, regardless of what is happening, "I must keep going." It is something that you cannot afford to lose or trade for anything.

An excellent example of that is a mother who has a child she loves so much and will do anything in her power to save that child. Develop a routine of writing a positive note to yourself in an area in your house or life that is visible to you, such as your bedroom, bathroom, refrigerator, or car. You can also write encouraging notes to yourself by identifying one or two things you know for sure that you are good at. Compliment yourself. Find the reason why you like to do them. It is a great exercise that has helped many people overcome low self-esteem, loneliness, and even rejection. Create a yearly calendar for yourself; it will motivate you to be inspired and even do things that you never did before.

Here are the four steps that can keep you encouraged in your journey.

Step 1 - Prayer

Prayer is a dialogue an individual has with God to communicate a personal request or acknowledge a petition. Therefore, prayer is the fuel that facilitates the engine of a human soul to connect with God in the spiritual realm. It helps to activate your blessing from heaven to come down.

In other words, prayer is a critical factor that helps one to live in the physical world and face life with confidence. Prayer will help you to avoid an unnecessary path. Having the wisdom of God can guide you to do not only what is right but also help you stay in alignment with your purpose.

Prayer helps you get a revelation. Having a revelation from God can make life much easier and save you a lot of money and time. When God reveals something to you, He wants you to follow a path that will lead you to your destination. Be open to and mindful of hearing the voice of God.

Step 2 - Perseverance

Perseverance is the audacity that one must accomplish something regardless of what obstacles come your way. Perseverance does not accept failure because when you want to go after something you want so badly, it does not matter what comes your way. Your motivation and desire to get to your destination will get you motivated to pursue your dreams. Remember your "WHY". Why do you want to embark on this journey? Perseverance allows you to see your future resolved.

After I returning to school to finish my degree back in 2019, I had everything mapped out in my mind that I was going back to finish my degree. I purchased my cap and gown. I bought myself four expensive gifts as a reward for finishing strong and having all A's. I visualized myself crossing the stage with my degree. I started manifesting everything that I wanted to happen. I prayed, meditated and manifested. Truth be told, on May 2021, I cross the stage with my degree. I create a quote that says "If you can dream it, you can become it".

However, perseverance and prayer work together as twin sisters because prayer is the gatekeeper of your destiny.

Step 3 - Mission

I want to encourage you to pursue your mission to fulfill an assignment, a burning desire to finish your career or your dream of becoming the next star. Become the person you are dreaming about. Become and do what you need to do to accomplish it. We need to fulfill the mission so the vision can come to pass. Therefore, stay encouraged and motivated. Before starting your journey, know that it will not be an easy road. Nevertheless, keep in mind that it will all be worth it.

Step 4 - Vision

A vision is something that you want to achieve, and it is tailored to your preferences. Your vision will never be something you cannot reach. Remember, if God can plant the desire in you, He will make provisions for you. Your vision should make you feel excited all the time because you are so curious about seeing the product of your hard work and efforts. Vision gives you a reason to live. Do not give up your dreams. You are what your generation is waiting for to revolutionize.

One of my favorite quotes I created is "***You have the power to live your vision now, just start acting like you already have it.***" You may have many ideas coming to mind, but if you do not have a vision, the ideas are irrelevant. The vision is like a plan that you draw even before you see the accurate results. It is like you are imagining getting there before even getting started. This is what is going to serve you as motivation.

Made in USA - Crawfordsville, IN
27903_9798425879905
03.09.2022 1620